THE OFFICIAL
CRYSTAL PALACE
ANNUAL 2018

CRYSTAL PALACE F.C.
1905

Written by James Bandy

Designed by Alice Lake-Hammond

A Grange Publication

© 2017. Published by Grange Communications Ltd., Edinburgh, under licence from Crystal Palace Football Club. Printed in the EU.

Every effort has been made to ensure the accuracy of information within this publication but the publishers cannot be held responsible for any errors or omissions. Views expressed are those of the author and do not necessarily represent those of the publishers or the football club. All rights reserved.

Special thanks to Ian King and Peter Hurn.

Photographs © Crystal Palace FC, Reuters, Press Association & Shutterstock

ISBN: 978-1-911287-86-5

CONTENTS

SEASON REVIEW 2016/17

WITH TRANSFER RECORDS SMASHED, A RELEGATION BATTLE, A NEW MANAGER AND ONE OF THE CRAZIEST GAMES IN PALACE'S HISTORY, THE 2016/17 SEASON CERTAINLY WASN'T BORING...

AUGUST

Hopes were high for the 2016/17 season, despite the previous campaign ending with just two wins from the last 21 games. Alan Pardew spent over £50 million on nine summer signings, including a record £32 million for Christian Benteke from Liverpool, England midfielder Andros Townsend and defender James Tomkins from West Ham. Following disappointing 1-0 defeats to West Brom and Spurs, The Eagles gained their first point of the season in the 1-1 draw with Bournemouth thanks to an injury-time goal by skipper Scott Dann. Progress in the EFL Cup was secured thanks to a 2-0 home win over Blackpool.

SEPTEMBER

Following a tough month for Eagles fans, September gave them hope for the season with three wins and a draw in the Premier League. A 2-1 away victory at newly-promoted Middlesbrough kick-started the season, before a 4-1 demolition of Stoke at Selhurst Park gave a glimpse of the team's potential. A trip to the North East followed to face struggling Sunderland, and hopes were high for three points. But following a disastrous start Palace found themselves 2-0 down courtesy of a Jermain Defoe brace, and staring at possible defeat. Second-half goals from Ledley and McArthur brought the scores level, before an injury-time strike from Benteke handed Palace the three points and gave the fans plenty to smile about on the long journey home. A creditable 1-1 draw at Goodison Park rounded off the month to leave Palace in 8th position on 11 points, and with one defeat in seven matches in all competitions.

OCTOBER

If The Eagles were flying high in September, they came back down to earth in October. It started with a 1-0 defeat at rivals West Ham, where Christian Benteke missed a penalty as well as a golden opportunity to equalise and there followed a 3-1 defeat at champions Leicester. The month ended with Liverpool coming to Selhurst Park in one of the most memorable games of the season. The first half saw three goals scored in less than six minutes, with Emre Can's opener cancelled out by James McArthur, only for Dejan Lovren to restore Liverpool's advantage. McArthur equalised again in the 33rd minute, only for Matip to score just before half-time to take The Reds into the break 3-2 up. Despite a better defensive display in the second half, Palace conceded a fourth without being able to score again themselves.

NOVEMBER

The month started with a trip to face Burnley at Turf Moor. Though both sides were on ten points, all of Burnley's had come at home, and it proved to be another tough afternoon. After being 0-2 down at half-time, a second-half comeback saw Pardew's side level the game at 2-2 with goals from Wickham and Benteke but, just as Eagles fans thought they'd earned a hard-fought point, Barnes scored a devastating winner in the 95th minute. Amazingly, Andros Townsend nearly levelled again straight afterwards, but his shot cannoned off the post and Palace left empty-handed. A 2-1 home defeat to Man City followed, before undoubtedly the craziest game of the season, if not for a number of years. The Eagles travelled to Swansea a point above the relegation zone, with The Swans rooted to the foot of the table. Zaha scored the opener for Palace after 19 minutes, before a Sigurdsson free-kick levelled the score. In the second half, the game exploded into life. Leroy Fer hit two quickfire goals to put Swansea 3-1 up, before goals from Tomkins, Zaha and Benteke netted to give Palace a 4-3 lead and on the verge of winning their first Premier League game for two months. But somehow, The Eagles managed to concede twice in injury-time to leave everyone completely devastated. Worse still, the result put them level on points with Hull in 18th and just three points off the bottom of the table. Things had to change – and fast.

SEASON REVIEW 2016/17

DECEMBER

Things did change in December – most notably the manager, as Alan Pardew was replaced by former England manager Sam Allardyce just before Christmas. A 3-0 home win over Southampton had papered over the cracks at the start of the month and a late equaliser salvaged a point at relegation rivals Hull. However, defeats to Manchester United and Chelsea left The Eagles in 17th position with one win from 11, one place and one point above the relegation zone, and the decision was taken to relieve Pardew of his duties. It wasn't taken lightly, but 26 points from 36 Premier League games in 2016 told its own story. Allardyce, looking for redemption after an all-too brief stint as England manager and with a track record of keeping clubs up, was an obvious choice. His first game in charge, the 1-1 draw with Watford on Boxing Day, was a decent start but showed the work that needed to be done. Could he be the man to do it?

JANUARY

A 2-0 defeat to Arsenal on New Year's Day was followed by another defeat to Swansea, before a number of players were rested for the trip to one of Allardyce's old clubs, Bolton, in the third round of the FA Cup. A 0-0 draw was played out, with Palace securing their place in the fourth round ten days later with a 2-1 victory at Selhurst Park. Back in the Premier League, The Eagles saw Zaha and Bakary Sako leave on African Cup of Nations duty, and it took its toll on the team. A 3-0 defeat against West Ham and a 1-0 defeat at home to Everton left Allardyce without a win in six games and no clean sheet in eight Premier League games. Thankfully, Zaha returned to the side in time for the game at Bournemouth, which they won 2-0, to give Big Sam his first win as Palace boss and the team some confidence going into February. A 3-0 defeat at home to Manchester City saw the FA Cup dream die, but with Premier League survival at stake, there weren't too many tears shed.

FEBRUARY

Any confidence gained from Bournemouth was undone in the very next game. Bottom of the table Sunderland, another of Big Sam's former clubs, arrived at Selhurst Park and Palace were well fancied to record back-to-back wins in the league for the first time since September. What happened sent a chill through every Palace fan. Kone gave The Black Cats the lead after nine minutes, but just as it looked as though The Eagles might go into the break one goal down at half-time, disaster struck. Ndong added a second after 43 minutes, before Jermain Defoe struck twice more in first-half injury-time to make it 0-4 at the break. No more goals were scored in the second half, but the damage had been done. It left Palace with eight defeats in nine home games, and five in a row. More worryingly, it saw them drop to 19th, with only a better goal difference keeping them off the foot of the table. A 1-0 defeat at Stoke the following week was their 16th of the season, but a 1-0 win at the end of February, where Mamadou Sakho made his Eagles debut on loan from Liverpool, lifted them out of the relegation zone and gave hope of better things to come.

MARCH

With the international break towards
the end of the month there were only
two Premier League games in March.
It allowed Big Sam time to work on
implementing his tactics and style,
and for the players to take it on board
and carry out the orders on the pitch. It
seemed to work. Palace travelled to the
West Midlands to face West Brom, who
were enjoying an incredible season and
pushing for a Europa League place. But
Palace won 2-0, securing only their fourth
clean sheet of the campaign. Wilfried
Zaha opened the scoring in the 55th
minute before Andros Townsend claimed
one of Palace's goals of the season, and
the BBC's Goal of the Month winner for
March. Picking the ball up deep in his own
half with just a few minutes to go, he ran
almost the full length of the pitch before
beating Gareth McAuley and firing in at
the near post. A 1-0 home win against
Watford, courtesy of a Troy Deeney own
goal, gave Palace a 100 per cent record
for the month, their third consecutive
win without conceding, and moved them
to the relative safety of 16th, four points
clear of the relegation zone.

APRIL

With seven Premier League matches, and games including Chelsea, Arsenal, Leicester, Liverpool and Spurs, April was the make-or-break month for The Eagles. They were given little hope by neutrals as they travelled to champions-elect Chelsea at the start of the month, but they produced arguably the result of the season with a superb 2-1 victory. After going 1-0 down on 5 minutes, Palace roared back to score twice in three minutes, with Christian Benteke's deft dink over Courtois the highlight. But a 3-1 defeat at Southampton followed, before The Eagles swept Arsenal aside 3-0 at Selhurst Park. The improvement was there for all to see, with Palace's defence tough and resilient, with Mamadou Sakho a giant in their backline. A 2-2 draw with Leicester followed after being 2-0 down, before the next game saw them make the trip to Anfield to face third-placed Liverpool. A win would take a huge leap towards survival, but this was going to be far from easy. Coutinho opened the scoring for the Reds, before Benteke equalised against his old club just before the break. In the second half, an entertaining game was won by that man Benteke, who headed in from six yards following a corner. The result put Palace on 38 points, seven clear of the relegation zone, and with six wins from eight Premier League games, their place in next season's top flight looked all but assured. Home defeats against Spurs and Burnley at the end of April took a little shine off the previous results, but with next season's Premier League status the priority, April was a great month for The Eagles.

MAY

Palace travelled to Manchester City in good spirits, but The Eagles, playing an unfamiliar 3-5-2 formation, conceded after just two minutes – and it got worse from there. A lacklustre display ended in a 5-0 defeat, their heaviest of the season and their third on the trot and left them with the possibility of needing one more win to secure safety. However, that was assured in the next game, an emphatic 4-0 win over Hull that assured Palace's safety and The Tigers' relegation. Zaha opened the scoring after just three minutes and Benteke made it two before half time, before late goals from Milivojevic and Van Aanholt put the gloss on an impressive display. A 2-0 defeat at Manchester United rounded off a campaign that saw Palace finish in 14th place on 41 points. But after a turbulent season at Selhurst Park, the chance for players and fans alike to recharge the batteries before another season in the Premier League was all important.

WORDSEARCH

CAN YOU FIND THE NAMES OF ALL THESE CRYSTAL PALACE LEGENDS?

```
I  W  S  I  E  E  O  A  O  D  C  C  P  P  P  R  U  E  A  U  A
C  N  R  A  Z  T  O  C  T  A  P  M  H  R  I  O  M  K  L  A  E
M  B  O  I  N  M  C  S  T  I  T  O  D  W  A  H  S  I  L  U  T
B  R  U  R  G  S  Q  S  E  S  P  U  F  A  H  I  P  N  I  U  A
I  R  E  O  E  H  O  D  M  P  U  G  T  A  W  A  F  K  S  R  C
C  Y  E  G  D  P  T  M  S  B  K  J  O  O  T  D  R  F  O  D  S
M  Y  T  B  D  M  S  A  F  O  D  R  A  B  M  O  L  R  N  U  C
U  B  A  T  M  O  Y  E  T  U  U  V  R  E  N  R  Y  B  Y  W  Y
L  C  Y  Y  S  E  R  A  U  T  P  E  H  E  I  U  D  I  U  P  E
L  E  L  D  E  R  K  S  E  I  R  F  F  E  J  A  M  D  J  E  D
I  A  O  R  O  X  U  C  A  N  N  O  N  F  A  U  O  O  O  G  E
N  M  R  E  F  R  A  H  Y  O  P  N  T  X  R  N  D  O  H  D  W
S  S  A  L  A  K  O  Y  E  W  N  D  N  P  B  O  M  W  N  I  D
G  N  O  L  E  R  E  E  D  L  C  R  H  N  R  S  N  L  S  R  J
I  C  C  I  D  A  E  Z  B  A  D  Y  R  X  I  N  O  E  O  R  E
I  A  F  R  E  E  D  M  A  N  X  N  B  Q  G  E  S  H  N  U  T
U  G  I  C  X  I  T  H  O  M  A  S  I  E  H  H  K  S  B  B  M
H  N  F  E  A  T  P  F  S  X  T  D  R  W  T  P  C  N  V  W  H
M  O  R  R  I  S  O  N  H  O  P  K  I  N  S  E  A  I  D  C  O
U  M  D  W  T  S  I  M  P  S  O  N  Y  N  U  T  J  H  L  O  E
P  U  E  N  O  T  P  N  Y  T  R  A  M  P  T  S  Q  E  J  V  X
```

Salako   Mullins   Bright   Rodger   Martyn   Taylor   Wright   Jeffries   Hopkin   Allison
Simpson   Swindlehurst   Stephenson   Freedman   Hinshelwood   Morrison   Lombardo
Jackson   Cannon   Burridge   Thomas   Johnson   Murphy   Kember   Sansom   Speroni
Harry   Shaw   Byrne   Long

CHECK THE SOLUTION ON PAGE 60

WHO ARE YA?

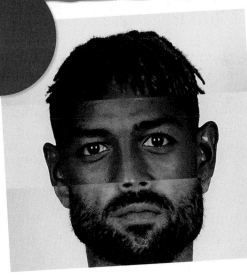

1

HAIR . . . .
EYES . . . .
CHIN . . . .

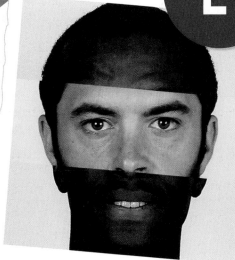

2

HAIR . . . .
EYES . . . .
CHIN . . . .

3

HAIR . . . .
EYES . . . .
CHIN . . . .

4

HAIR . . . .
EYES . . . .
CHIN . . . .

WE'VE JUMBLED UP THE FACES OF SOME
PALACE STARS. CAN YOU TELL WHO THE THREE
PLAYERS ARE IN EACH OF THESE PICTURES?

CHECK THE SOLUTION ON PAGE 61

11 WILFRIED ZAHA

6 SCOTT DANN

THE ULTIMATE GUIDE TO... WILFRIED ZAHA!

FIND OUT EVERYTHING YOU NEED TO KNOW – AND MORE – ABOUT THE EAGLES' TALISMAN!

WILF... ON THE PITCH

DRIBBLING

Being blessed with great balance, quick feet and having a number of tricks in his locker means Wilf is a superb dribbler. Every time he gets the ball, he's looking to run with it. The winger executed the most dribbles in the Premier League in 2016-17 and was the most fouled player too. Zaha running at top speed is a defender's worst nightmare!

SHOOTING

Zaha can shoot with either foot. It doesn't matter whether on his right or left, he gets the ball out of his feet and gets his shot off. He probably doesn't score as many goals as he would like, or that his all-round play deserves, but his seven Premier League goals last season was his best return yet, and when he does net, they're usually ones to remember!

SPEED

In a word, frightening. Even more frightening is the fact Zaha has the ability to run with the ball at his feet almost as fast as without it, and is able to twist and turn without losing speed. His reactions are razor sharp and he's fast over short distances, but when he reaches top speed defenders are left choking on his dust!

TRICKS

Zaha's got more tricks than Dynamo! It's the most striking part of his game, and the fact he can execute so many tricks so well means defenders never know what he's going to do next. Flip-flaps, stepovers, drag-backs, nutmegs, chopsticks, round the world, Cruyff turns – Wilf's got the lot!

PASSING

This is another area of Wilf's game that has improved in the last couple of years. He has always liked to play little one-twos with team-mates to get past defenders, but his final ball has come on loads too. The winger himself said he needed to improve his end product, be it a cross or shot, and his passing – especially short passes.

CROSSING

Zaha is from the new generation of wingers who generally prefer to cut inside before playing a team-mate in or squaring the ball, but he's worked hard on improving his crossing too. He seems as happy taking a defender on down the outside before popping the ball up for Palace forwards to attack as he does cutting inside.

DEFENDING

With his incredible skills you could almost forgive him for not wanting to defend, but this side of Zaha's game has come on loads in the last couple of years. He works his socks off for the team, tracking back and trying to get a foot in before starting attacks with his fearsome pace and trickery.

STRENGTH

Despite only being 5'10" and weighing 66kgs, Wilf is a top athlete and very strong for his size. He's not afraid to take a challenge, and even though he receives more than his fair share of rough stuff from opponents, he's never bullied by them. His strength also allows him to hold off defenders, either with his back to goal or when running alongside them.

WHAT THEY SAY:

" *What he has in his skills I think he is a lot like, if I had to give an example, for me it's Neymar. He also has the quick feet and he's gone. Very skinny, so fast, every touch, every pass.*"

PALACE MANAGER FRANK DE BOER

" *Wilfried is a unique type of person, a unique type of player. He doesn't conform to any rules or regulations.*"

SHAUN DERRY, FORMER PALACE CAPTAIN

" *Have I seen anyone like him? No. Not in my whole career. When I was growing up, you had the Harlem Globetrotters. Well, he can do all of those things with a ball at his feet.*"

FORMER PALACE MANAGER IAN HOLLOWAY

" *I've managed Tevez, Mascherano, Teddy Sheringham, Joey Barton, Jermain Defoe, and I'd put Wilf right up there with all of those players.*"

FORMER MANAGER ALAN PARDEW

NOW TURN OVER FOR WILF OFF THE PITCH!

WILF... OFF THE PITCH!

JAN 2013

FAMILY

Wilf and his family moved to England from the Ivory Coast when he was just four years old. They settled in Thornton Heath with his mum and dad, five brothers and three sisters, and he says his dad was his biggest inspiration growing up. When he's not playing football he loves spending time with them and his girlfriend and young son.

MONEY

He might be a superstar Premier League footballer, but Wilf isn't driven by money. When he could afford it, one of the first things he did was buy a house for his parents. He also donates ten per cent of his salary to charities in the UK and back in the Ivory Coast to help those less fortunate than himself. What a ledge!

WILFRIED ZAHA TIMELINE...

NOV 1992	1997	2004	MAR 2010
Dazet Wilfried Armel Zaha is born in Abidjan, Ivory Coast on November 10, 1992.	Wilf and his family move to England. Living in Thornton Heath in London, young Wilf attends Whitehorse Manor Junior School and then Selsdon High School.	At the age of 12, Wilf is spotted by Palace scouts and starts attending their academy.	On March 27, 2010, the 17-year-old makes his Palace debut against Cardiff, coming on with ten minutes to go in a 2-1 defeat.

CLOTHES

The Palace hero is massively into fashion and loves spending time looking for clothes. But a while ago, annoyed that he couldn't find the gear he was looking for, his girlfriend suggested he started making them himself. So he did. Well, sort of - he launched his own label, Long Live, named after his Instagram account!

SOCIAL MEDIA

Zaha loves social media, and can be found on Twitter and Instagram (@wilfriedzaha and @longlivezaha). He's always posting cool pics on Instagram and has around 35,000 followers, while he has over 750,000 followers on Twitter. Go check him out!

MUSIC

Wilf is well into his music, and hip-hop in particular. Growing up he used to listen to stuff his brothers were into, like Tupac, 50 Cent, Dr. Dre and Snoop Dogg. He still loves a bit of Kanye West, but he's also a big fan of local talent, and reckons artists like Stormzy, Krept & Konan and Section Boyz are decent too.

FAITH

He doesn't like to shout about it because he says everyone should make their own decisions, but Wilf is a big believer in Christianity. He wasn't too keen when he started going to church at the age of eight or nine, but he now prays regularly, through the good times and the bad, and says his faith keeps him strong.

MAR 2012	NOV 2012	JAN 2013	MAY 2013	MAY 2013
Wilf is voted the Football League's Young Player of the Year.	Makes his senior England debut, coming on as a substitute in a 4-2 defeat to Sweden in Stockholm.	Manchester United pay Palace £15 million to sign Zaha, and then loan him straight back to The Eagles to help their promotion push.	Scores both goals in the second leg of the Championship play-off semi-final against rivals Brighton to book Palace's place at Wembley.	Wins the penalty in the play-off final against Watford, which Kevin Phillips scores, to send The Eagles back to the Premier League.

WILF... THE STATS

PL - ALL TIME STATS
Games: 115
Goals: 13
Wins: 34
Draws: 25
Losses: 56

ALL-TIME PL GOALS
Goals per match: 0.11
Headers: 0
Right foot: 11
Left foot: 2

ALL-TIME PL ATTACKING
Assists: 13
Passes: 1820
Passes per match: 15.83
Big chances created: 18
Crosses: 358
Cross accuracy: 21%
Through balls: 10
Accurate long balls: 49

MAY 2016

QUICK STAT
Zaha completed 147 dribbles in the Premier League last season – that's more than any other player!

WILFRIED ZAHA TIMELINE...

AUG 2013
Makes his Manchester United debut in the 2-0 Community Shield win over Wigan

JAN 2014
After struggling to get game time at Manchester United, he moves to Premier League strugglers Cardiff until the end of the season.

AUG 2014
Palace agree a deal with Manchester United to take Zaha on loan for the season.

FEB 2015
At the end of the transfer window, makes his move back to The Eagles permanent, signing for an undisclosed fee.

MAY 2016
Plays the whole 120 minutes in the FA Cup final against former club Manchester United but can't prevent a 2-1 defeat.

AWARDS
PALACE PLAYER OF THE YEAR:
2015-16, 2016-17
PALACE YOUNG PLAYER OF THE YEAR:
2010-11, 2011-12
FOOTBALL LEAGUE YOUNG PLAYER OF
THE YEAR: 2012-13

ALL-TIME PL DISCIPLINE

Yellow cards: 15

Red cards: 0

Fouls: 147

Offsides: 25

ALL-TIME PL DEFENDING

Tackles: 183

Tackle success: 79%

Blocked shots: 41

Interceptions: 88

Clearances: 28

Recoveries: 591

Duels won: 888

Successful 50/50s: 394

ALL-TIME PL SHOOTING

Shots: 135

Shots on target: 48

Shot accuracy: 36%

Woodwork: 4

SEASON BY SEASON

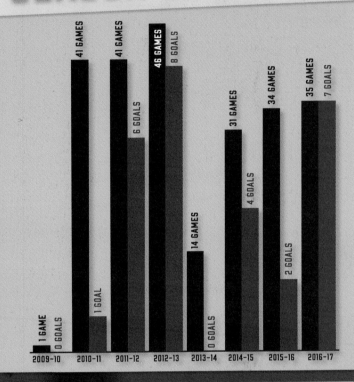

2009-10	1 GAME	0 GOALS
2010-11	41 GAMES	1 GOAL
2011-12	41 GAMES	6 GOALS
2012-13	46 GAMES	8 GOALS
2013-14	14 GAMES	0 GOALS
2014-15	31 GAMES	4 GOALS
2015-16	34 GAMES	2 GOALS
2016-17	35 GAMES	7 GOALS

MAY 2016

Wins the Crystal Palace Player of the Year award for the first time.

NOV 2016

Wilf commits to play for the Ivory Coast. Despite having played twice for England, the fact they were friendlies allows him to do this.

JAN 2017

Makes his Ivory Coast debut against Togo in the 2017 African Cup of Nations.

MAY 2017

Scores the goal against Hull that mathematically secures Palace's top-flight status, and is named Palace's Player of the Year for the second year running.

MAY 2017

Commits his future to Palace by signing a new five-year deal with the club.

CRYSTAL PALACE...
STAT ATTACK!

CHECK OUT THESE MIND-BLOWING STATS ABOUT THE EAGLES!

141 — Up to the end of last season, defender Joel Ward held the record for the most Premier League appearances by a Palace player with 141!

49 — The player with the most Premier League wins in a Palace shirt was held by Jason Puncheon, who had claimed three points 49 times with The Eagles!

660 — Legendary Eagles centre-back Jim Cannon holds the record for the most Crystal Palace appearances, playing for the club 660 times between 1973 and 1988!

312 — The club had played 312 Premier League games before the start of the 2017-18 season, winning 86, drawing 78 and losing 148!

254 — Goalkeeper John Jackson holds the record for the most consecutive appearances for The Eagles – he played a staggering 254 games on the trot!

165 — Goal king Peter Simpson holds the record for the most goals in a Palace shirt, hitting 165 during his time at the club between 1929 and 1935!

54 — The Scottish striker also holds the record for the most Palace goals in a single season, hitting an incredible 54 strikes in all competitions in 1930-31 including 46 in the league!

21 — That's how many league goals striker Andy Johnson hit for The Eagles during the 2004-05 season – that's a record for a Palace player in the top flight!

49 — In 1992-93, the first season of the Premiership, Palace finished on 49 points but were still relegated – that's still a Premier League record!

90

Palace's highest ever points total is 90, when they won the Championship during the 1993-94 season!

3

In 1989-1990, the club finished third in Division One behind champions Arsenal and runners-up Liverpool – that's the club's highest top-flight finish!

329

Before the start of the 2017-18 season, The Eagles had scored a total of 329 Premier League goals over eight seasons!

0.19

And when you take into account they'd taken 1763 shots to score that number of goals, their goals to shots ratio is just under 0.19, or a goal from just over every five shots!

But if you then consider that 573 of those shots had been on target, that means they've scored every 1.74 shots that have been on goal!

0

Palace didn't receive a red card in the Premier League last season – only Chelsea, Tottenham, Liverpool and Swansea can say the same!

6

Palace's fastest-ever goal was scored by Keith Smith away at Derby on December 12, 1964, when he found the net after just six seconds!

1.3

That was Palace's average goals per game in the Premier League in 2016-17, which was better than their all-time Premier League average of 1.05!

9

On October 10, 1959, the club recorded its biggest ever win when they put nine goals past Barrow in a 9-0 win in the old fourth division!

17

The most consecutive wins The Eagles have recorded is 17, when they won every game from October 14, 1905 to April 7, 1906!

51,482

The record attendance for a Palace match was the 51,482 that saw them play Burnley on May 11, 1979 which saw them promoted back to the first division!

20 QUESTIONS

HOW MUCH DO YOU KNOW ABOUT THE EAGLES? TAKE THIS QUIZ TO FIND OUT!

1. IN WHICH YEAR WAS THE CLUB FORMED?
   a) 1901
   b) 1905
   c) 1909

2. WHO IS THE CLUB'S ALL-TIME RECORD TRANSFER?

3. IN WHICH YEAR DID THEY MOVE TO THEIR CURRENT SELHURST PARK HOME?
   a) 1920
   b) 1922
   c) 1924

4. WHICH PLAYER IS THEIR ALL-TIME RECORD GOALSCORER?

5. FROM WHICH CLUB DID THE EAGLES SIGN SCOTT DANN?

6. PALACE'S FIRST KIT WAS CLARET AND BLUE BECAUSE IT WAS DONATED TO THEM BY WEST HAM. TRUE OR FALSE?

7. WHICH PLAYER HOLDS THE RECORD FOR THE MOST PALACE APPEARANCES?

8. WHO SCORED THE WINNING GOAL FROM THE PENALTY SPOT WHEN PALACE BEAT WATFORD IN THE 2013 CHAMPIONSHIP PLAY-OFF FINAL?

9. IN WHICH YEAR DID WILFRIED ZAHA MAKE HIS DEBUT FOR THE CLUB?

10. BOSS RONALD DE BOER HAS WON THE WORLD CUP WITH HOLLAND. TRUE OR FALSE?

11. HOW MANY TIMES HAVE PALACE PLAYED IN AN FA CUP FINAL?

12. WHAT IS THE CURRENT CAPACITY OF SELHURST PARK?
   a) 25,456
   b) 26,456
   c) 27,456

13. IN 1993, PALACE WERE RELEGATED FROM THE PREMIER LEAGUE WITH A TOTAL OF 49 POINTS, WHICH IS STILL A RECORD. TRUE OR FALSE?

14. WHAT IS PALACE'S HIGHEST TOP-FLIGHT FINISH?

15. FROM WHICH CLUB DID THE EAGLES SIGN GOAL HERO IAN WRIGHT?
   a) Greenwich Borough
   b) Dulwich Hamlet
   c) Hendon

16. HOW MUCH DID PALACE PAY NEWCASTLE UNITED TO SIGN ANDROS TOWNSEND IN THE SUMMER OF 2016?

17. FROM WHICH COUNTRY DOES PALACE DEFENDER PAPE SOUARE COME FROM?

18. WHAT IS LOAN STAR RUBEN LOFTUS-CHEEK'S SQUAD NUMBER THIS SEASON FOR PALACE?

19. HOW MANY TIMES HAVE THE CLUB BEEN CHAMPIONS OF THE ENGLISH SECOND TIER?

20. PALACE SIGNED SERBIAN STAR LUKA MILIVOJEVIC FROM WHICH CLUB?
   a) Anderlecht
   b) Olympiakos
   c) Red Star Belgrade

CHECK THE ANSWERS ON PAGE 60

FACE IN THE CROWD

CAN YOU SPOT THE NINE CRYSTAL PALACE PLAYERS HIDING IN AMONGST THE FANS?
THEY'RE ALL IN HERE SOMEWHERE!

Luka Milivojevic

Scott Dann

Jason Puncheon

Yohan Cabaye

Ruben Loftus-Cheek

Christian Benteke

James Tomkins

Wilfried Zaha

James McArthur

CHECK THE SOLUTION ON PAGE 61

PALACE'S ALL-TIME BEST

XI

THERE HAVE BEEN SOME LEGENDARY PLAYERS TO HAVE PULLED ON A PALACE SHIRT IN THEIR 112-YEAR HISTORY, AND IT GOT US THINKING. IF YOU HAD TO COME UP WITH A STARTING LINE-UP OF THE GREATEST PLAYERS EVER IN EACH POSITION, WHO WOULD MAKE THE TEAM? CHECK OUT THE CONTENDERS HERE, AND THEN DECIDE YOUR ALL-STAR LINE-UP AT THE END!

ALL STATS CORRECT TO START OF 2017/18 SEASON

GOALKEEPERS

JOHN JACKSON 1962-73
Games: 388
The keeper made 222 consecutive starts and was an ever-present in 1968-69 as the club were promoted to the top-flight for the first time in their history.

JOSHUA JOHNSON 1907-19
Games: 295
Johnson spent 12 years at Palace and made 295 appearances for the club, who were then in the Southern League, up to the start of the First World War.

NIGEL MARTYN 1989-96
Games: 349
Martyn became the first £1 million keeper when Palace signed him from Bristol Rovers in 1989, and the stopper won three England caps while at the club.

JULIAN SPERONI 2004-present
Games: 390
The Palace legend holds the record for the most appearances by a keeper, and he's won Player of the Year and Supporters' Player of the Year four times each!

GABOR KIRALY 2004-07
Games: 111
Hungarian stopper Kiraly only spent three seasons at Selhurst Park but quickly became a cult hero with his legendary grey tracksuit bottoms!

DANNY BUTTERFIELD 2002-10
Games: 269
Goals: 10
The versatile full-back became a big fans' favourite and scored Palace's fastest-ever hat-trick – a perfect hat-trick too – in 6 minutes 48 seconds against Wolves in 2010 as a makeshift striker!

NATHANIEL CLYNE 2008-12
Games: 137
Goals: 1
Clyne came through the ranks at Palace and in 2010-11 became the youngest player in the Football League to play every game that season, also winning the Player of the Year award.

PAUL HINSHELWOOD 1971-83
Games: 319
Goals: 28
'Doris' as he was called by fans, was a Croydon lad who spent 12 years at the club. He was Palace's Player of the Year two seasons in a row when they were in the top flight between 1979 and 1981.

JOEL WARD 2012-present
Games: 186
Goals: 4
Wardy signed from Portsmouth in 2012 and his goal-line clearance in the 2013 play-off final against Watford will long be remembered. He also holds the record for most Premier League appearances for Palace.

MARC EDWORTHY 1995-98
Games: 151
Goals: 1
He only spent three seasons at the club, but Edworthy got The Eagles promoted back to the Premier League in his first season and was Supporters' Player of the Year in his second.

CHRIS COLEMAN 1991-95

Games: 190

Goals: 16

The central defender could also play as a makeshift striker, and had a goal record of one in nine. Two of his four seasons were in the Premier League and he won his first Wales caps while at the club.

SCOTT DANN 2014-present

Games: 118

Goals: 14

Dann joined from Blackburn in January 2014 and soon showed everyone what he was about, winning the Player of the Year award in 2015 and the Players' Player of the Year in 2016.

RICHARD SHAW 1987-95

Games: 268

Goals: 3

After coming through the youth system, Shaw became a key part of the side that reached the FA Cup final and finished third in the Premier League, Palace's highest ever finish.

GARETH SOUTHGATE 1989-95

Games: 191

Goals: 22

After coming through the ranks at Palace, Southgate, who started his career in central midfield, took over the captaincy and led the club to the First Division title in 1993-94.

ANDY THORN 1989-94

Games: 168

Goals: 7

Thorn was a tough central defender who took no prisoners, which made him a big hit with fans. He shored up the defence, playing in the 1990 FA Cup final and keeping the club in the top flight for four years.

DEFENDERS

ERIC YOUNG 1990-95
Games: 204
Goals: 17
'The Ninja' didn't join until he was 30 but quickly became a legend, his partnership with Andy Thorn helping Palace to finish third in 1991 and he was always a goal threat from set-pieces.

JIM CANNON 1971-88
Games: 660
Goals: 36
Palace legend Jim Cannon was a classy centre-back who captained the club for ten years. He holds the record for appearances – and only four of those appearances were as a sub!

ALAN STEPHENSON 1962-68
Games: 185
Goals: 13
Stephenson came through the ranks at Palace and became captain at the age of 19. Dominant in the air and a solid defender, West Ham signed him for a club record £80,000 fee in 1968.

PETER RAMAGE 2011-12/2012-15
Games: 67
Goals: 4
Despite only playing 67 games for the club, Ramage became a big fans' favourite for his all-action displays and helped the club win promotion to the Premier League in 2013.

TERRY LONG 1955-70
Games: 480
Goals: 18
Defender Long made 480 appearances during a 15-year career at the club, once making 214 consecutive appearances and helping the club to promotion in 1961 and 1964.

DAMIEN DELANEY 2012-present
Games: 189
Goals: 7
The tough Republic of Ireland defender joined in 2012 from Ipswich and has become a big favourite, helping the club back to the Premier League in his first season.

DEAN GORDON 1991-98
Games: 241
Goals: 23
The Croydon-born left-back started his career at Palace and fans loved him for his barnstorming attacking runs and spectacular strikes.

KENNY SANSOM 1975-80
Games: 197
Goals: 4
One of England's finest left-backs and arguably Palace's greatest ever player, Samson joined as a trainee, won Player of the Year as a 17-year-old and made nearly 200 appearances in five years before moving to Arsenal.

PATRICK VAN AANHOLT 2017-present
Games: 11
Goals: 2
PVA made such a good impression after joining the club in January 2017, that he could turn out to be a Palace legend!

JONATHAN PARR 2011-14
Games: 101
Goals: 2
With superb fitness and an incredible work ethic, the Norway international was a big fans' favourite, winning Player of the Year in 2012 and helping the club to the Premier League the following season.

JOHN HUMPHREY 1990-95
Games: 203
Goals: 2
Another member of the 1991 team that finished third, Humphrey joined from rivals Charlton but won fans over with his classy displays at right-back and scored one of the best-ever goals against Wolves in 1993!

MIDFIELDERS

YANNICK BOLASIE 2012-16
Games: 144
Goals: 13
Bolasie became a huge fans' favourite with his ridiculous skill, tricks and dribbling, and became the first Palace player to score a Premier League hat-trick with a treble at Sunderland in 2015.

VINCE HILAIRE 1976-84
Games: 293
Goals: 36
Vince joined Palace as a trainee and made his debut as a 17-year-old. A quick and tricky winger, he was part of the famous 'Team of the 80s' and is remembered fondly by fans.

ATTILIO LOMBARDO 1997-99
Games: 48
Goals: 10
'The Bald Eagle' was only at Palace for a season and a half after signing from Juventus in 1997, but the Italy star's skill and work-rate still saw him named in Palace's Centenary XI.

JOHN SALAKO 1986-1995
Games: 273
Goals: 34
A fast and tricky winger, Salako started his career with the club and went on to make 273 appearances over nine years, including an FA Cup final and part of the team that finished third in 1990-91.

PETER TAYLOR 1973-76
Games: 142
Goals: 39
A gifted winger, Taylor spent three years at Palace, winning Player of the Year twice and making four England appearances while at the club, scoring two goals.

WILFRIED ZAHA 2010-13/2015-present

Games: 258

Goals: 34

A star of the current team, Wilf came through the ranks to star for The Eagles, scoring two goals in the 2013 play-off semi-final against Brighton and briefly joining Manchester United before returning to Palace in 2015.

DARREN AMBROSE 2009-12

Games: 124

Goals: 37

Ambrose scored the goal against Sheffield Wednesday that kept Palace up in 2010 and he loved a long-range screamer, just like the strike at Manchester United in the 2011-12 League Cup.

ANDY GRAY 1984-87/1989-92

Games: 242

Goals: 51

Gray joined the club at the age of 11 and was an absolute beast who could play as well. He scored in the 4-3 FA Cup semi-final win over Liverpool, was part of the legendary squad of 1990-91 and even played once for England.

MICHAEL HUGHES 2003-07

Games: 141

Goals: 10

Hughes joined from Wimbledon in 2003 and quickly became a fans' favourite with his excellent vision, pinpoint passing and cultured left foot. He was named captain in 2004-05.

MILE JEDINAK 2011-16

Games: 179

Goals: 10

Another fans' favourite for his tough, all action displays, Mile scored the goal that secured Palace's play-off place in 2013, was Player of the Year that season and then nearly played every minute in the Premier League in 2013-14.

MIDFIELDERS

STEVE KEMBER 1963-71/1978-80
Games: 291
Goals: 38
After coming through the ranks, Kember scored the goal that saw Palace promoted to the top flight for the first time. He left for Chelsea in 1971, but returned seven years later.

JASON PUNCHEON 2013-14/2014-present
Games: 149
Goals: 16
An all-action player who can operate on either wing or in behind the striker, Puncheon joined on loan in 2013 before making the deal permanent in 2014 and has become a big favourite.

AKI RIIHILAHTI 2001-06
Games: 178
Goals: 14
Everyone's favourite Finn, the hard-working Riihilahti had a flag with 'AKI 15' in the Holmesdale and holds the record for gaining the most caps for his country while at Palace.

GEOFF THOMAS 1987-93
Games: 249
Goals: 35
Thomas won the Supporters' Player of the Year award in his first season, helped Palace to promotion the next and was a key member of the 1990 FA Cup final side and the one that finished third in 1991.

DAVID HOPKIN 1995-97/2001-02
Games: 127
Goals: 33
The Scottish international enjoyed two spells at Selhurst Park but will always be remembered for his 90th-minute play-off final winner against Sheffield United in 1997 to secure a place in the Premier League.

RAY HOUGHTON 1995-97
Games: 86
Goals: 8
Although he arrived towards the end of his career the former Liverpool and Republic of Ireland star was a real class act, bringing calmness, composure and a wealth of experience.

GEORGE CLARKE 1925-33
Games: 299
Goals: 106
Although a winger, Clarke scored 106 goals in his eight years at the club, but was best known as a creator, supplying chances for the prolific Peter Simpson up front.

JERRY MURPHY 1976-85
Games: 269
Goals: 25
Murphy started his career at Palace, winning the FA Youth Cup in 1977 and 1978 before helping the club to promotion in his first full season. He also won the Player of the Year award in 1983.

DON ROGERS 1972-74
Games: 83
Goals: 30
Rogers only spent two seasons at the club, but what an impact he had. Quick, two-footed and elegant, he scored 1973's Goal of the Season against Stoke City and was incredible in the 5-0 demolition of Manchester United.

ANDROS TOWNSEND 2016-present
Games: 40
Goals: 3
Another member of the current squad, Andros loves to get on the ball and dribble, and scored one of the goals of the season in 2016-17 with his solo run and finish away at West Brom.

VICTOR MOSES 2007-10
Games: 69
Goals: 11
Moses came through the youth ranks and exploded on to the first-team scene, but his Palace career was cut short when he was sold to Wigan.

FORWARDS

CHRIS ARMSTRONG 1992-95
Games: 136
Goals: 58
The striker joined The Eagles from Millwall for the first ever Premier League season, and smashed in an impressive 23 goals despite the club's relegation.

CHRISTIAN BENTEKE 2016-present
Games: 40
Goals: 17
The Belgium international arrived from Liverpool for a record £27 million, but has repaid a big chunk of the fee with the goals that helped keep Palace up last season.

MARK BRIGHT 1986-92
Games: 286
Goals: 113
Half of the formidable Bright-Wright partnership in the late 80s and early 90s, Brighty was quick, hard-working and was a sweet striker of the ball. A true Palace great.

JOHNNY BYRNE 1956-62/1967-68
Games: 259
Goals: 101
'Budgie' Byrne, so called because he never stopped talking, hit 30 goals for the club in 1961 as they won promotion to the Third Division, and returned for a second spell in 1967.

DOUGIE FREEDMAN 1996-97/2000-08
Games: 368
Goals: 108
Another player to have two spells at the club, Freedman also managed Palace too. He was a massive hero with fans, and his goal against Stockport saved The Eagles from relegation to the third tier in 2001.

ANDY JOHNSON 2002-06/2014-15
Games: 161
Goals: 85
After joining from Birmingham, the striker soon announced himself with a hat-trick against Brighton and another in the next match! He scored 32 goals as Palace were promoted in 2004 and his 21 Premier League goals in 2004-05 is still a Palace record.

CLINTON MORRISON 1997-02/2005-08
Games: 316
Goals: 113
Morrison scored on his debut, played for the club for free when they were in administration, was top scorer for four seasons in a row and is Palace's joint-third highest goalscorer of all-time.

PETER SIMPSON 1929-35
Games: 195
Goals: 165
Palace's all-time record scorer, Simpson scored a hat-trick on his debut before going on to score 19 in total, a Palace record. His 54 goals for the club in 1930-31 is also a club best, but a knee injury sadly cut his career short in 1935.

DAVE SWINDLEHURST 1973-80
Games: 276
Goals: 81
Swindlehurst started his career at Palace, and scored the goal against Burnley in front of a record crowd that saw The Eagles promoted to the First Division. A real cult hero.

IAN WRIGHT 1985-91
Games: 277
Goals: 117
Wrighty joined Palace at the age of 21, and was a goalscoring machine. Pacy, brave and with a real eye for goal, he became Palace's post-war top goalscorer and second on the all-time list. He was voted in the Centenary XI and voted Player of the Century.

NOW IT'S YOUR TURN!

YOU'VE READ ALL ABOUT SOME OF PALACE'S GREATEST EVER PLAYERS, SO NOW WE WANT YOU TO CHOOSE YOUR ALL-TIME FAVOURITE STARTING LINE-UP. GRAB A PEN AND SOME FAMILY, FRIENDS, WHOEVER, AND LET THE DEBATES BEGIN!

MY ALL-TIME CRYSTAL PALACE XI

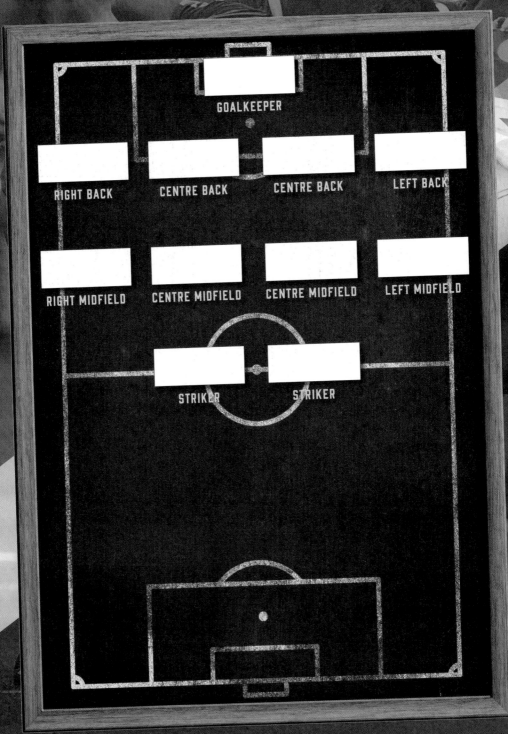

42 JASON PUNCHEON

DESIGN YOUR OWN PALACE KIT!

THERE'S NOTHING BETTER THAN SEEING THE EAGLES' LATEST KIT, BUT WHY NOT HAVE A GO AT CREATING YOUR OWN CRYSTAL PALACE HOME AND AWAY KITS?

CHECK OUT SOME OF THE CLASSIC AND CRAZY KITS BELOW, AND THEN HAVE A GO YOURSELF! GRAB YOUR COLOURED PENS OR PENCILS AND DESIGN NEW KITS FOR THE EAGLES!!

1972

1988

1999

2013

2008

AWAY

CRYSTAL PALACE'S...
LEAGUE OF NATIONS!

PALACE'S SQUAD IS MADE UP OF PLAYERS WHO REPRESENT 14 DIFFERENT COUNTRIES. FIND OUT WHERE EACH ONE HAILS FROM AND A BIT MORE ABOUT THEIR NATION!

THE NETHERLANDS
Capital: Amsterdam
Population: 17 million
Top teams: Ajax, PSV, Feyenoord
Palace players: Patrick van Aanholt, Jairo Riedewald, Tim Fosu-Mensah

SCOTLAND
Capital: Edinburgh
Population: 5.3 million
Top teams: Celtic, Rangers, Aberdeen
Palace players: James McArthur

IRELAND
Capital: Dublin
Population: 5.78 million
Top teams: Dundalk, Cork City
Palace players: Damien Delaney

WALES
Capital: Cardiff
Population: 3.1 million
Top teams: Cardiff, Swansea, TNS
Palace players: Wayne Hennessey

EUROPE

ENGLAND
Capital: London
Population: 53 million
Top teams: Chelsea, Man. United, Man. City
Palace players: Joel Ward, James Tomkins, Scott Dann, Martin Kelly, Andros Townsend, Sullay Kaikai, Jason Puncheon, Jordon Mutch, Ruben Loftus-Cheek, Connor Wickham, Freddie Ladapo

BELGIUM
Capital: Brussels
Population: 11.35 million
Top teams: Anderlecht, Club Brugge, Genk
Palace players: Christian Benteke, Jason Lokilo

FRANCE
Capital: Paris
Population: 67 million
Top teams: PSG, Monaco, Lyon
Palace players: Yohan Cabaye, Mamadou Sakho

SERBIA
Capital: Belgrade
Population: 7.1 million
Top teams: Partizan Belgrade, Red Star Belgrade
Palace players: Luka Milivojevic

SENEGAL
Capital: Dakar
Population: 15.4 million
Top teams: AS Douanes, ASC Diaraf
Palace players: Pape Souare

MALI
Capital: Bamako
Population: 18 million
Top teams: Djoliba Athletic Club, Stade Malien
Palace players: Bakary Sako

SOUTH KOREA
Capital: Seoul
Population: 51.3 million
Top teams: Seongnam FC, Pohang Steelers
Palace players: Chung-Yong Lee

ARGENTINA
Capital: Buenos Aires
Population: 43.9 million
Top teams: Boca Juniors, River Plate
Palace players: Julian Speroni

GHANA
Capital: Accra
Population: 28.2 million
Top teams: Asanti Kotoko, Hearts of Oak
Palace players: Jeffrey Schlupp

IVORY COAST
Capital: Abidjan
Population: 23.7 million
Top teams: ASEC Mimosas, AS Tanda
Palace players: Wilfried Zaha

REST OF THE WORLD!

PALACE'S STARS OF THE FUTURE!

THE EAGLES ARE FAMOUS FOR PRODUCING LOADS OF TOP PLAYERS THROUGH THEIR ACADEMY. MEET THE LATEST BATCH OF YOUNGSTERS AIMING TO BE THE NEXT ZAHAS, SAMSONS, SALAKOS AND GRAYS!

JASON LOKILO

POSITION: MIDFIELD
COUNTRY: BELGIUM
BORN: 17.09.1998
SIGNED: 25.09.2015

2016/17 STATS:
U23S – 13 APPEARANCES, 1 GOAL
U18S – 16 APPEARANCES, 5 GOALS

The former Anderlecht academy member started training with The Eagles in the summer of 2015 and signed his first professional deal the following September. Skilful and keen to take on defenders, the Belgian right-winger can also play in a more attacking role, which saw him net regularly for the under-18s. Last season, he shared time between the development and academy teams, and featured in most first-team matches during 2016-17 pre-season.

JOSEPH HUNGBO

POSITION: MIDFIELD
COUNTRY: ENGLAND
BORN: 15.01.2000
SIGNED: 01.12.2016

2016-17 STATS:
U23S - 2 APPEARANCES,
0 GOALS
U18S - 24 APPEARANCES,
1 GOAL

The winner of the club's Under 9-16 Player of the Year award in 2015-16, Hungbo came through the Oasis Shirley Park programme. A rapid left-winger with outrageous skill and a powerful strike, he made his under-18s debut at 15 and scored the winner in a 1-0 victory at home to Ipswich. Rumour has it both England and Nigeria are trying to convince Joseph to commit to them. His performances last season saw him earn a couple of call-ups to the development team towards the end of the campaign, and he'll be looking to add to those this season.

TARIQ OSSAI

POSITION: DEFENDER
COUNTRY: ENGLAND
BORN: 14.10.1999
SIGNED: 20.11.2016

2016-17 STATS:
U18S - 27 APPEARANCES,
2 GOALS

A versatile defender who captained both the Under-16s and the Under-18s over the past two seasons, Tariq signed a scholarship in the summer of 2016 after impressing in his first few games at academy level in 2015-16. He featured in pre-season for the first-team and looks to have a great future ahead of him.

PALACE'S STARS OF THE FUTURE!

KIAN FLANAGAN

POSITION: MIDFIELD
COUNTRY: REPUBLIC OF IRELAND
BORN: 29.08.1999
SIGNED: 01.07.2016

2016-17 STATS:
U23S – 14 APPEARANCES, 1 GOAL
U18S – 14 APPEARANCES, 5 GOALS

A creative attacking midfielder, Flanagan has been tipped for big things at Palace after making his development team debut aged just 15 at the end of the 2014-15 season. Since then, the Republic of Ireland international has split his time between the Under-18s and Under-23s, with his displays last season seeing him named as Palace's Scholar of the Year.

LEVI LUMEKA

POSITION: MIDFIELD
COUNTRY: ENGLAND
BORN: 05.09.1998
SIGNED: 01.07.2015

2016-17 STATS:
U23S – 18 APPEARANCES, 6 GOALS
U18S – 8 APPEARANCES, 5 GOALS

After finishing top scorer for the academy side in 2015-16, Levi repeated the feat with the development side last term despite spending time with the Under-18s. Prolific in the younger age groups, the pacy winger is strong on the ball, tricky, and has lots of skill, and can also play as a striker.

10 ANDROS TOWNSEND

WORD-FIT

CAN YOU FIT THESE EAGLES PLAYERS FROM THE 2016-17
SEASON INTO THIS GRID?

BENTEKE
BOATENG
CABAYE
CAMPBELL
DANN
DELANEY
FLAMINI
FRYERS
HENNESSEY
KAIKAI
KELLY
LEDLEY
LEE
MANDANDA
MCARTHUR
MILIVOJEVIC
MUTCH
PUNCHEON
SAKHO
SAKO
SCHLUPP
SOUARE
SPERONI
TOMKINS
TOWNSEND
VAN AANHOLT
WICKHAM
ZAHA

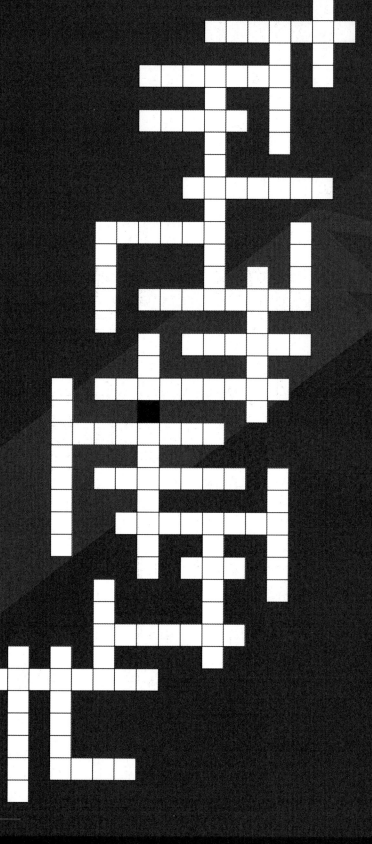

CHECK THE SOLUTION ON PAGE 61

SPOT THE DIFFERENCE

THERE ARE SIX DIFFERENCES BETWEEN THESE TWO PICTURES OF THE TEAM HUDDLE. CAN YOU SPOT THEM ALL?

CHECK THE SOLUTION ON PAGE 60

THE A TO Z OF PALACE!

LEARN EVERYTHING YOU NEED TO KNOW ABOUT OUR GREAT CLUB THROUGH EVERY LETTER OF THE ALPHABET!

A

Is for Aston Villa who, strangely enough, played a big part in the club's formation. Palace's first Secretary-Manager, E.F. Goodman, came from the Birmingham club and took the club's kit with him, so the first Crystal Palace teams turned out in claret shirts with blue sleeves and white shorts!

Is for Brighty, who joined in 1986 from Leicester and went on to become a club legend. Alongside Ian Wright, he formed the most lethal duo Crystal Palace has ever seen. He was the perfect foil for the free-scoring Wright, but he was a quality goalscorer in his own right, notching 113 goals in 286 appearances.

B

C

Is for Cannon, Jim Cannon. It had to be. After joining as an apprentice, the Scot clocked up nearly 200 more appearances than nearest rival Terry Long and seemed to be an almost ever-present in The Eagles' defence for 16 years. Always in the right place at the right time, and with an ability to make it look all so easy.

Is for Dave Clark Five. They wrote Glad All Over, the Palace anthem that's sung before and after every home game. The band performed on the pitch back in February 1968, and the club loved it so much they adopted it as their song and it's stuck ever since!

D

E

Is for Eagles. Not the nickname but Pete, the ultra-cool mascot, his wife Alice, and Kayla, the American bald eagle that flies around Selhurst before every game. Did you know that Kayla was born in Canada and has appeared on the cover of a Kings of Leon album?

F

Is for FA Cup. Palace have reached the final twice in their history, first in 1990 and again in 2016, where they faced Manchester United both times. In 1990 Ian Wright made it 2-2 just three minutes after coming on as a sub and then gave Palace the lead in extra-time, before Mark Hughes took it to a replay, which The Eagles lost 1-0.

G

Is for Glaziers, Palace's original nickname. When the club was formed in 1905, it was a nod to the original 'Crystal Palace' amateur team that was formed in 1861 (but had nothing to do with the current club) who were full-time glaziers at the palace!

H

Is for Holmesdale End, home of much of the singing and on its day, one of the loudest and best atmospheres in the Premier League. As for the stand itself, it replaced the old Holmesdale terrace in 1994-95 and is the newest stand at Selhurst, seating 5,341 in the lower tier and 2,806 in the upper.

I

Is for the Intertoto Cup, the competition Palace played in the only time they've played in a European competition. In July 1998 they took on Turkish side Samsunspor, entering the competition in the third round, but lost both legs 2-0 to crash out.

J

Is for John Bostock, Palace's youngest ever player. The winger made his Eagles debut in 2007 at just 15 years and 287 days in a tie with Watford. The youngster made only three more appearances before joining Tottenham in a £700,000 deal.

K

Is for kits. There has been loads of different colours, and some real crackers! Claret shirts and blue sleeves, claret and blue stripes, blue with claret stripes, white with a claret and blue stripe – there's been loads! The club changed to red and blue in 1973, but still had a couple of years with the iconic white shirt with red and blue sash.

L

Is for Jack Little, the oldest player ever to represent the club. In seven years at Palace the Northumberland-born full-back played 261 games, his last being against Gillingham in April 1926 at the age of 41 years and 68 days!

M

Is for Malcolm Allison, the manager who did so much to form the club as it is today. In an attempt to reinvent the club, he changed their nickname to The Eagles after Benfica, to broaden appeal and make the club sound more intimidating, and switched the club colours to red and blue stripes, with a nod to Barcelona!

N

Is for the new boys Palace signed last summer. The Eagles snapped up 21-year-old Holland international defender Jairo Riedewald from Ajax for £9 million, as well as Tim Fosu-Mensah and Ruben Loftus-Cheek on season-long loans.

O

Is for one-club players. There's hardly any of them any more, but The Eagles were lucky enough to have two pretty much one after the other. Defender Terry Long made 480 appearances between 1955 and 1969, and just three years later, Jim Cannon came through the ranks to make his debut and go on to make 660 appearances between 1972 and 1988!

P

Is for play-offs. Dreaded by many, but Palace seem to love them! They've won the play-offs four times, against Blackburn, West Ham, Sheffield United and Watford, and have only suffered one defeat in the final, against Leicester in 1996.

Q

Is for Gerry Queen, the Scottish striker who scored against Manchester United in their first-ever top-flight game in 1969. But equally as memorable are some of the amazing newspaper headlines he produced including 'Queen in brawl at Palace', 'Queen is king at the Palace' and 'Gerryatrick'!

R

Is for rivalries. Millwall and Charlton are big, but the fiercest by far has to be Brighton. In 1976 the two teams met in the first round of the FA Cup. In the second replay, Brighton scored a penalty but the referee ordered it to be retaken. The retake was saved, Palace went on to win 1-0 and a fierce rivalry was born.

S

Is for Peter Simpson, the club's greatest ever goalscorer. The Scot, who signed for the club from Kettering in 1929, only spent five years at the club before moving to West Ham, but in that time he scored 165 goals in 195 games, hit 20 hat-tricks, and in 1930-31 scored 54 goals – and all of them are still Palace records over 80 years later!

T

Is for tracksuit bottoms. Well, Gabor Kiraly's anyway. The former 'keeper and his grey pants became cult heroes at Selhurst Park. Kiraly said he wore them at his former club and they brought him luck, so he kept wearing them. Weirdly, he once ditched them for a game against Chelsea and Palace lost 4-1, so he could be right!

Is for UEFA Cup, the competition Palace could have played in the season after their third-placed finish in 1990-91. But because Liverpool's six-year ban from European competition was lifted at the end of the season, and they finished second, it was them who played in the UEFA Cup instead. Gutting!

U

V

Is for venues. The Eagles hold the record for winning the play-offs at the most different venues, having done it at Selhurst Park, the old Wembley, the Millennium Stadium and the new Wembley. Get in!

Is for Wait, Arthur Wait. A former director, chairman and Life President, he has a stand named in his honour. He's also famous for being so outraged at a famous English club's fee for playing a friendly to celebrate the new floodlights, he said, 'We could get Real Madrid for that!' so he did!

W

X

Is for X-rated. That's what some of the treatment dished out to flying winger Wilfried Zaha is! The Ivory Coast wizard is a marked man in the Premier League and was fouled 121 times last season, a record since the stat has been recorded. He also topped the list last season as well!

Is for yo-yo club, during the Premier League era at least. In 25 years of the PL, Palace have been promoted five times and relegated five, which is more than any other club. But the good news is that before 2013, the club had never lasted more than a season in the Premier League, so four years and counting is pretty good!

Y

Z

Isn't for Zaha! Admit it, you thought it would be, didn't you? Well that's why it's for Fan Zhiyi, who became the first Chinese star ever to play in the Premier League when he joined Palace in 1998. He went on to captain the club and was a big favourite with fans.

BEFORE THEY WERE... FAMOUS!

CHECK OUT THESE PALACE STARS BEFORE THEY HIT THE BIG-TIME!

JOEL WARD (2009)
Wardy looks about 12 in this pic from his Pompey days!

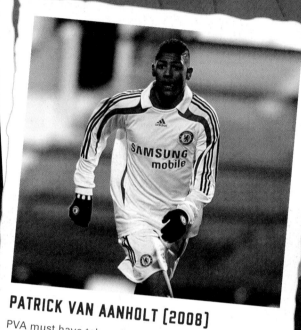

PATRICK VAN AANHOLT (2008)
PVA must have taken the wrong kit – it's massive on him!

YOHAN CABAYE (2004)
The France star looked slick even back then!

JASON PUNCHEON (2006)
Has Punch even changed at all?

JAMES MCARTHUR (2008)

Jimmy Mac looks a bit scared – it must be his fringe!

MARTIN KELLY (2009)

Martin looks like someone out of a 90s indie band!

CONNOR WICKHAM (2009)

Has Connor just got out of bed?

SCOTT DANN (2007)

You wouldn't want to mess with this fella!

DAMIEN DELANEY (2001)

How young does DD look in this pic?

WILFRIED ZAHA (2010)

Can you believe this was Wilf just seven years ago? Crazy!

CRYSTAL PALACE FIRST-TEAM SQUAD 2017/18

GOALKEEPERS

JULIAN SPERONI
Date of birth: 18.05.1979
Country: Argentina
Height: 186cm
Signed: July 2004 from Dundee
Fee: £750,000
Palace appearances/goals: 390/0

WAYNE HENNESSEY
Date of birth: 24.01.1987
Country: Wales
Height: 198cm
Signed: January 2014 from Wolves
Fee: £1.6million
Palace appearances/goals: 77/0

DEFENDERS

JOEL WARD
Date of birth: 29.10.1989
Country: England
Height: 188cm
Signed: May 2012 from Portsmouth
Fee: £400,000
Palace appearances/goals: 186/5

PATRICK VAN AANHOLT
Date of birth: 29.08.1990
Country: Netherlands
Height: 176cm
Signed: January 2017 from Sunderland
Fee: £14million
Palace appearances/goals: 11/2

JAMES TOMKINS
Date of birth: 29.03.1989
Country: England
Height: 192cm
Signed: June 2016 from West Ham
Fee: £10million
Palace appearances/goals: 27/3

SCOTT DANN
Date of birth: 14.02.1987
Country: England
Height: 188cm
Signed: January 2014 from
Blackburn
Fee: Undisclosed
Palace appearances/goals:
118/15

JEFFREY SCHLUPP
Date of birth: 23.12.1992
Country: Ghana
Height: 178cm
Signed: January 2017 from
Leicester
Fee: £12 million
Palace apps/goals: 16/0

PAPE SOUARE
Date of birth: 06.06.1990
Country: Senegal
Height: 178cm
Signed: January 2015 from
Lille
Fee: Undisclosed
Palace appearances/goals:
55/0

TIMOTHY FOSU-MENSAH
Date of birth: 02.01.1998
Country: Holland
Height: 190cm
Signed: August 2017 from
Man. United
Fee: Loan
Palace apps/goals: 0/0

DAMIEN DELANEY
Date of birth: 20.07.1981
Country: Republic of Ireland
Height: 191cm
Signed: August 2012 from
Ipswich
Fee: Free
Palace appearances/goals:
189/7

MARTIN KELLY
Date of birth: 27.04.1990
Country: England
Height: 191cm
Signed: August 2014 from
Liverpool
Fee: £2million
Palace appearances/goals:
85/1

JAIRO RIEDEWALD
Date of birth: 09.09.1996
Country: Holland
Height: 182cm
Signed: July 2017 from Ajax
Fee: £7.9 million
Palace apps/goals: 0/0

MAMADOU SAKHO
Date of birth: 13.02.1990
Country: France
Height: 187cm
Signed: August 2017 from
Liverpool
Fee: £26 million
Palace apps/goals: 0/0

LUKA MILIVOJEVIC

Date of birth: 07.04.91
Country: Serbia
Height: 186cm
Signed: 31.01.17 from
Olympiakos
Fee: £16 million
Palace apps/goals: 14/2

YOHAN CABAYE

Date of birth: 14.01.1986
Country: France
Height: 174cm
Signed: July 2015 from PSG
Fee: Undisclosed
Palace appearances/goals:
75/10

RUBEN LOFTUS-CHEEK

Date of birth: 23.01.1996
Country: England
Height: 191cm
Signed: July 2017 from
Chelsea
Fee: Loan
Palace appearances/goals: 0/0

ANDROS TOWNSEND

Date of birth: 16.07.1991
Country: England
Height: 181cm
Signed: July 2016 from
Newcastle
Fee: £13million
Palace appearances/goals:
40/3

WILFRIED ZAHA

Date of birth: 10.11.1992
Country: Ivory Coast
Height: 180cm
Signed: February 2015 from
Manchester United
Fee: Undisclosed
Palace appearances/goals:
258/36

CHUNG-YONG LEE

Date of birth: 02.07.1998
Country: South Korea
Height: 180cm
Signed: Feb 2015 from Bolton
Fee: Undisclosed
Palace appearances/goals:
40/2

JAMES MCARTHUR

Date of birth: 07.10.1987
Country: Scotland
Height: 178cm
Signed: September 2014
Fee: Undisclosed
Palace appearances/goals:
95/9

JORDON MUTCH

Date of birth: 02.12.1991
Country: England
Height: 184cm
Signed: January 2015 from
QPR
Fee: Undisclosed
Palace apps/goals: 40/0

SULLAY KAIKAI
Date of birth: 26.08.1995
Country: England
Height: 182cm
Signed: July 2013
Fee: N/A
Palace appearances/goals: 5/1

BAKARY SAKO
Date of birth: 26.04.1988
Country: Mali
Height: 183cm
Signed: August 2015
Fee: Free agent
Palace appearances/goals: 31/2

JASON PUNCHEON
Date of birth: 26.06.1986
Country: England
Height: 173cm
Signed: January 2014 from Southampton
Fee: £1.75million
Palace appearances/goals: 149/16

CRYSTAL PALACE FIRST-TEAM SQUAD 2017/18

FORWARDS

CHRISTIAN BENTEKE
Date of birth: 03.12.1990
Country: Belgium
Height: 190cm
Signed: August 2016 from Liverpool
Fee: £32million
Palace appearances/goals: 40/17

FREDDIE LADAPO
Date of birth: 01.02.1993
Country: England
Height: 183cm
Signed: August 2016 from Margate
Fee: Undisclosed
Palace apps/goals: 0/0

CONNOR WICKHAM
Date of birth: 31.03.1993
Country: England
Height: 191cm
Signed: August 2015
Fee: Undisclosed
Palace appearances/goals: 34/10

QUIZ ANSWERS

WORDSEARCH (P12)

```
I W S I E E O A O D C C P P P R U E A U A
C N R A Z T O C T A P M H R I O M K L A E
M B O I N M C S T I T O D W A H S I L U T
B R U R G S Q S E S P U F A H I N I U A
I R E O E H O D M P U G T A W A F K S R C
C Y E G D P T M S B K J O O T D R F O D S
M Y T B D M S A F O D R A B M O L R N U C
U B A T M O Y E T U U V R E N R Y B Y W Y
L C Y Y S E R A U T P E H E I U D I U P E
L E L D E R K S E I R F F E J A M D J E D
I A O R O X U C A N N O N F A U O O O G E
N M R E F R A H Y O P N T X R N D O H D W
S S A L A K O Y E W N D N P B O M W N I D
G N O L E R E E D L C R H N R S N L S R J
I C C I D A E Z B A D Y R X I N O E O R E T
I A F R E E D M A N X N B Q G E S H N U T
U G I C X I T H O M A S I E H H K S B B M
H N F E A T P F S X T D R W T P C N V W H
M O R R I S O N H O P K I N S E A I D C O
U M D W T S I M P S O N Y N U T J H L O E
P U E N O T P N Y T R A M P T S Q E J V X
```

SPOT THE DIFFERENCE (P49)

20 QUESTIONS (P24)

1. B) 1905
2. CHRISTIAN BENTEKE (£32 MILLION)
3. C) 1924
4. PETER SIMPSON (165 GOALS)
5. BLACKBURN
6. FALSE – IT WAS DONATED BY ASTON VILLA
7. JIM CANNON – 660 APPEARANCES
8. KEVIN PHILLIPS
9. 2010 V CARDIFF
10. FALSE
11. TWICE – 1990 AND 2016
12. A) 25,456
13. TRUE
14. THIRD (1990–91)
15. A) GREENWICH BOROUGH
16. £13 MILLION
17. SENEGAL
18. 8
19. TWICE – 1978-79, 1993-94
20. B) OLYMPIAKOS

FACE IN THE CROWD [P25]

WHO ARE YA? [P13]

1.
HAIR: Zaha
EYES: van Aanholt
CHIN: Delaney

2.
HAIR: Puncheon
EYES: Tomkins
CHIN: Kaikai

3.
HAIR: Dann
EYES: Loftus-Cheek
CHIN: Kelly

4.
HAIR: Hennessey
EYES: Benteke
CHIN: Cabaye

WORD-FIT [P48]